I0504592

Risks Facing
The
Global Economy

By

Roshdy Ebrahim, Ph.D

2020

Risks facing the global economy

Contents

Chapter 1
How we can predict the next financial crisis [1]

Once upon a time we lived in an economy of financial growth and prosperity. This was called the Great Moderation, the misguided belief by most economists, policymakers and central banks that we have transformed into a new world of never-ending growth and prosperity. This was seen by robust and steady GDP growth, by low and controlled inflation, by low unemployment, and controlled and low financial volatility.

But the Great Recession in 2007 and 2008, the great crash, broke this illusion. A few hundred billion dollars of losses in the financial sector cascaded into five trillion dollars of losses in world GDP and almost $30 trillion losses in the global stock market.

So, the understanding of this Great Recession was that this was completely

---

[1] Didier Sornette: risk economist

surprising, this came out of the blue, this was like the wrath of the gods. There was no responsibility. So, as a reflection of this, we started the Financial Crisis Observatory. We had the goal to diagnose in real time financial bubbles and identify in advance their critical time.

What is the underpinning, scientifically, of this financial observatory? We developed a theory called "dragon-kings." Dragon-kings represent extreme events which are of a class of their own. They are special. They are outliers. They are generated by specific mechanisms that may make them predictable, perhaps controllable.

Consider the financial price time series, a given stock, your perfect stock, or a global index. You have these up-and-downs. A very good measure of the risk of this financial market is the peaks-to-valleys that represent a worst-case scenario when you bought at the top and sold at the bottom. You can look at the statistics, the frequency of the occurrence of peak-to-valleys of different sizes, which is represented in this graph. Now, interestingly, 99 percent of the peak-to-valleys of different amplitudes can be represented by a universal power law represented by this red line here. More interestingly, there are outliers, there are exceptions which are above this red line, occur 100 times more frequently, at least, than the extrapolation would predict them to occur based on the calibration of the 99 percent remaining peak-to-valleys. They are due to trenchant dependencies such that a loss is followed by a loss which is followed by a loss which is followed by a loss. These kinds of dependencies are largely missed by standard risk management tools, which ignore them and see lizards when they should see dragon-kings. The root mechanism of a dragon-king is a slow maturation towards instability, which is the bubble, and the climax of the bubble is often the crash. This is similar to the slow heating of water in this test tube reaching the boiling point, where the instability of the water occurs and you have the phase transition to vapor. And this process, which is absolutely non-linear -- cannot be predicted by standard techniques -- is the reflection of a collective emergent behavior which is fundamentally endogenous. So, the cause of the crash, the cause of the crisis has to be found in an inner instability of the system, and any tiny perturbation will make this instability occur.

Now, some of you may have come to the mind that is this not related to the black swan concept you have heard about frequently? Remember, black swan is this rare bird that you see once and suddenly shattered your belief that all swans should be white, so it has captured the idea of unpredictability, unknowability, that the extreme events are fundamentally unknowable. Nothing can be further from the dragon-king concept I propose, which is exactly the opposite, that most extreme events are actually knowable and predictable. So, we can be empowered and take responsibility and make predictions about them. So, let's have my dragon-king burn this black swan concept.

There are many early warning signals that are predicted by this theory. Let me just focus on one of them: the super-exponential growth with positive feedback. What does it mean? Imagine you have an investment that returns the first-year five percent, the second-year 10 percent, the third-year 20 percent, the next year 40 percent. Is that not marvelous? This is a super-exponential growth. A standard exponential growth corresponds to a constant growth rate, let's say, of 10 percent The point is that, many times during bubbles, there are positive feedbacks which can be of many times, such that previous growths enhance, push forward, increase the next growth through this kind of super-exponential growth, which is very trenchant, not sustainable. And the key idea is that the mathematical solution of this class of models exhibit finite-time singularities, which means that there is a critical time where the system will break, will change regime. It may be a crash. It may be just a plateau, something else. And the key idea is that the critical time, the information about the critical time is contained in the early development of this super-exponential growth.

We have applied this theory early on, that was our first success, to the diagnostic of the rupture of key elements on the iron rocket. Using acoustic emission, you know, this little noise that you hear a structure emit, sing to you when they are stressed, and reveal the damage going on, there's a collective phenomenon of positive feedback, the more damage gives the more damage, so you can actually predict, within, of course, a probability band, when the rupture will occur.

Perhaps more surprisingly, the same type of theory applies to biology and medicine, parturition, the act of giving birth, epileptic seizures. From seven months of pregnancy, a mother starts to feel episodic precursory contractions of the uterus that are the sign of these maturations toward the instability, giving birth to the baby, the dragon-king. So, if you measure the precursor signal, you can actually identify pre- and post-maturity problems in advance. Epileptic seizures also come in a large variety of size, and when the brain goes to a super-critical state, you have dragon-kings which have a degree of predictability and this can help the patient to deal with this illness. We have applied this theory to many systems, landslides, glacier collapse, even to the dynamics of prediction of success: blockbusters, YouTube videos, movies, and so on. But perhaps the most important application is for finance, and this theory illuminates, I believe, the deep reason for the financial crisis that we have gone through. This is rooted in 30 years of history of bubbles, starting in 1980, with the global bubble crashing in 1987, followed by many other bubbles. The biggest one was the "new economy" Internet bubble in 2000, crashing in 2000, the real estate bubbles in many countries, financial derivative bubbles everywhere, stock market bubbles also everywhere, commodity and all bubbles, debt and credit bubbles -- bubbles, bubbles, bubbles.

We had a global bubble. This is a measure of global overvaluation of all markets, expressing what I call an illusion of a perpetual money machine that suddenly broke in 2007.

The problem is that we see the same process, in particular through quantitative easing, of a thinking of a perpetual money machine nowadays to tackle the crisis since 2008 in the U.S., in Europe, in Japan. This has very important implications to understand the failure of quantitative easing as well as austerity measures as long as we don't attack the core, the structural cause of this perpetual money machine thinking.

Now, these are big claims. Why would you believe me? Well, perhaps because, in the last 15 years we have come out of our ivory tower, and started to publish ex ante -- and I stress the term ex ante, it means "in advance" — before the crash confirmed the existence of the bubble or the financial excesses. These are a few of the major bubbles that we have lived through in recent history. Again, many interesting stories for each of them. Let me tell you just one or two stories that deal with massive bubbles.

We all know the Chinese miracle. This is the expression of the stock market of a massive bubble, a factor of three, 300 percent in just a few years. In September 2007, I was invited as a keynote speaker of a macro hedge fund management conference, and I showed to the conference a prediction that by the end of 2007, this bubble would change regime. There might be a crash. Certainly not sustainable. Now, how do you believe the very smart, very motivated, very informed macro hedge fund managers reacted to this prediction? You know, they had made billions just surfing this bubble until now. They told me, "Didier, yeah, the market might be overvalued, but you forget something. There is the Beijing Olympic Games coming in August 2008, and it's very clear that the Chinese government is controlling the economy and doing what it takes to also avoid any wave and control the stock market."

Three weeks after my presentation, the markets lost 20 percent and went through a phase of volatility, upheaval, and a total market loss of 70 percent until the end of the year.

So how can we be so collectively wrong by misreading or ignoring the science of the fact that when an instability has developed, and the system is ripe, any perturbation makes it essentially impossible to control?

The Chinese market collapsed, but it rebounded. In 2009, we also identified that this new bubble, a smaller one, was unsustainable, so we published again a prediction, in advance, stating that by August 2009, the market will correct, will not continue on this track. Our critics, reading the prediction, said, "No, it's not possible. The Chinese government is there. They have learned their lesson. They will control. They want to benefit from the growth." Perhaps these critics have not learned their lesson previously. So, the crisis did occur. The market corrected.

The same critics then said, "Ah, yes, but you published your prediction. You influenced the market. It was not a prediction."

Maybe I am very powerful then. Now, this is interesting. It shows that it's essentially impossible until now to develop a science of economics because we are sentient beings who anticipate and there is a problem of self-fulfilling prophesies.

So, we invented a new way of doing science. We created the Financial Bubble Experiment. The idea is the following. We monitor the markets. We identify excesses, bubbles. We do our work. We write a report in which we put our prediction of the critical time. We don't release the report. It's kept secret. But with modern encrypting techniques, we have a hash, we publish a public key, and six months later, we release the report, and there is authentication. And all this is done on an international archive so that we cannot be accused of just releasing the successes.

Let me tease you with a very recent analysis. 17th of May, 2013, just two weeks ago, we identified that the U.S. stock market was on an unsustainable path and we released this on our website on the 21st of May that there will be a change of regime. The next day, the market started to change regime, course. This is not a crash. This is just the third or fourth act of a massive bubble in the making. Scaling up the discussion at the size of the planet, we see the same thing. Wherever we look, it's observable: in the biosphere, in the atmosphere, in the ocean, showing these super-exponential trajectories characterizing an unsustainable path and announcing a phase transition. This diagram on the right shows a very beautiful compilation of studies suggesting indeed that there is a nonlinear -- possibility for a nonlinear transition just in the next few decades.

So, there are bubbles everywhere. From one side, this is exciting for me, as a professor who chases bubbles and slays dragons, as the media has sometimes called me.

But can we really slay the dragons? Very recently, with collaborators, we studied a dynamical system where you see the dragon-king as these big loops and we were able to apply tiny perturbations at the right times that removed, when control is on, these dragons.

"Gouverner, c'est prévoir." Governing is the art of planning and predicting. But is it not the case that this is probably one of the biggest gaps of mankind, which has the responsibility to steer our societies and our planet toward sustainability in the face of growing challenges and crises?

But the dragon-king theory gives hope. We learn that most systems have pockets of predictability. It is possible to develop advance diagnostics of crises so that we can be prepared, we can take measures, we can take responsibility, and so that never again will extremes and crises like the Great Recession or the European crisis take us by surprise.

Chapter2
What we learned from teetering on the fiscal cliff [2]

a friend of mine who's a political scientist, he told me several months ago exactly what this month would be like. He said, you know, there's this fiscal cliff coming, it's going to come at the beginning of 2013. Both parties absolutely need to resolve it, but neither party wants to be seen as the first to resolve it. Neither party has any incentive to solve it a second before it's due, so he said, December, you're just going to see lots of angry negotiations, negotiations breaking apart, reports of phone calls that aren't going well, people saying nothing's happening at all, and then sometime around Christmas or New Year's, we're going to hear, "Okay, they resolved everything." He told me that a few months ago. He said he's 98 percent positive they're going to resolve it, and I got an email

---

)[2] Adam Davidson: co-host and co-creator of planet money.

from him today saying, all right, we're basically on track, but now I'm 80 percent positive that they're going to resolve it.

And it made me think. I love studying these moments in American history when there was this frenzy of partisan anger, that the economy was on the verge of total collapse.

The most famous early battle was Alexander Hamilton and Thomas Jefferson over what the dollar would be and how it would be backed up, with Alexander Hamilton saying, "We need a central bank, the First Bank of the United States, or else the dollar will have no value. This economy won't work," and Thomas Jefferson saying, "The people won't trust that. They just fought off a king. They're not going to accept some central authority." This battle defined the first 150 years of the U.S. economy, and at every moment, different partisans saying, "Oh my God, the economy's about to collapse," and the rest of us just going about, spending our bucks on whatever it is we wanted to buy.

To give you a quick primer on where we are, a quick refresher on where we are. So, the fiscal cliff, I was told that that's too partisan a thing to say, although I can't remember which party it's supporting or attacking. People say we should call it the fiscal slope, or we should call it an austerity crisis, but then other people say, no, that's even more partisan. So, I just call it the self-imposed, self-destructive arbitrary deadline about resolving an inevitable problem. And this is what the inevitable problem looks like. So, this is a projection of U.S. debt as a percentage of our overall economy, of GDP. The light blue dotted line represents the Congressional Budget Office's best guess of what will happen if Congress really doesn't do anything, and as you can see, sometime around 2027, we reach Greek levels of debt, somewhere around 130 percent of GDP, which tells you that sometime in the next

20 years, if Congress does absolutely nothing, we're going to hit a moment where the world's investors, the world's bond buyers, are going to say, "We don't trust America anymore. We're not going to lend them any money, except at really high interest rates." And at that moment our economy collapses. But remember, Greece is there today. We're there in 20 years. We have lots and lots of time to avoid that crisis, and the fiscal cliff was just one more attempt at trying to force the two sides to resolve the crisis.

Here's another way to look at exactly the same problem. The dark blue line is how much the government spends. The light blue line is how much the government gets in. And as you can see, for most of recent history, except for a brief period, we have consistently spent more than we take in. Thus, the national debt. But as you can also see, projected going forward, the gap widens a bit and raises a bit, and this graph is only through

2021. It gets really, really ugly out towards 2030.

And this graph sort of sums up what the problem is. The Democrats, they say, well, this isn't a big deal. We can just raise taxes a bit and close that gap, especially if we raise taxes on the rich. The Republicans say, hey, no, no, we've got a better idea. Why don't we lower both lines? Why don't we lower government spending and lower government taxes, and then we'll be on an even more favorable long-term deficit trajectory? And behind this powerful disagreement between how to close that gap, there's the worst kind of cynical party politics, the worst kind of insider baseball, lobbying, all of that stuff, but there's also this powerfully interesting, respectful disagreement between two fundamentally different economic philosophies.

And I like to think, when I picture how Republicans see the economy, what I picture is just some amazingly well-engineered machine, some perfect machine. Unfortunately, I picture it made in Germany or Japan, but this amazing machine that's constantly scouring every bit of human endeavor and taking resources, money, labor, capital, machinery, away from the least productive parts and towards the more productive parts, and while this might cause temporary dislocation, what it does is it builds up the more productive areas and lets the less productive areas fade away and die, and as a result the whole system is so much more efficient, so much richer for everybody. And this view generally believes that there is a role for government, a small role, to set the rules so people aren't lying and cheating and hurting each other, maybe, you know, have a police force and a fire department and an army, but to have a very limited reach into the mechanisms of this machinery.

And when I picture how Democrats and Democratic-leaning economists picture this economy, most Democratic economists are, you know, they're capitalists, they believe, yes, that's a good system a lot of the time. It's good to let markets move resources to their more productive use. But that system has tons of problems. Wealth piles up in the wrong places. Wealth is ripped away from people who shouldn't be called unproductive. That's not going to create an equitable, fair society. That machine doesn't care about the environment, about racism, about all these issues that make this life worse for all of us, and so the government does have a role to take resources from more productive uses, or from richer sources, and give them to other sources. And when you think about the economy through these two different lenses, you understand why this crisis is so hard to solve, because the worse the crisis gets, the higher the stakes are, the more each side thinks they know the answer and the other side is just going to ruin everything.

And I can get really despairing. I've spent a lot of the last few years really depressed about this, until this year, I learned something that I felt really excited about. I feel like it's really good news, and it's so shocking, I don't like saying it, because I think people won't believe me. But here's what I learned. The American people, taken as a whole, when it comes to these issues, to fiscal issues, are moderate, pragmatic centrists. And I know that's hard to believe, that the American people are moderate, pragmatic centrists. But let me explain what I'm thinking.

When you look at how the federal government spends money, so this is the battle right here, 55 percent, more than half, is on Social Security, Medicare, Medicaid, a few other health programs, 20 percent defense, 19 percent discretionary, and six percent interest. So, when we're talking about cutting government spending, this is the pie we're talking about, and Americans overwhelmingly, and it doesn't matter what party they're in, overwhelmingly like that big 55 percent chunk. They like Social Security. They like Medicare. They even like Medicaid, even though that goes to the poor and indigent, which you might think would have less support. And they do not want it fundamentally touched, although the American people are remarkably comfortable, and Democrats roughly equal to Republicans, with some minor tweaks to make the system more stable.

Social Security is fairly easy to fix. The rumors of its demise are always greatly exaggerated. So gradually raise Social Security retirement age, maybe only on people not yet born. Americans are about 50/50, whether they're Democrats or Republicans.

Reduce Medicare for very wealthy seniors, seniors who make a lot of money. Don't even eliminate it. Just reduce it. People generally are comfortable with it, Democrats and Republicans.

Raise medical health care contributions? Everyone hates that equally, but Republicans and Democrats hate that together.

And so, what this tells me is, when you look at the discussion of how to resolve our fiscal problems, we are not a nation that's powerfully divided on the major, major issue. We're comfortable with it needing some tweaks, but we want to keep it. We're not open to a discussion of eliminating it.

Now there is one issue that is hyper-partisan, and where there is one party that is just spend, spend, spend, we don't care, spend some more, and that of course is Republicans when it comes to military defense spending. They way outweigh Democrats. The vast majority want to protect military defense spending. That's 20 percent of the budget, and that presents a more difficult issue. I should also note that the [discretionary] spending, which is about 19 percent of the budget, that is Democratic and Republican issues, so you do have welfare, food stamps, other programs that tend to be popular among Democrats, but you also have the farm bill and all sorts of Department of Interior inducements for oil drilling and other things, which tend to be popular among Republicans.

Now when it comes to taxes, there is more disagreement. That's a more partisan area. You have Democrats overwhelmingly supportive of raising the income tax on people who make 250,000 dollars a year, Republicans sort of against it, although if you break it out by income, Republicans who make less than 75,000 dollars a year like this idea. So basically, Republicans who make more than 250,000 dollars a year don't want to be taxed. Raising taxes on investment income, you also see about two thirds of Democrats but only one third of Republicans are comfortable with that idea.

This brings up a really important point, which is that we tend in this country to talk about Democrats and Republicans and think there's this little group over there called independents that's, what, two percent? If you add Democrats, you add Republicans, you've got the American people. But that is not the case at all. And it has not been the case for most of modern American history. Roughly a third of Americans say that they are Democrats. Around a quarter say that they are Republicans. A tiny little sliver calls themselves libertarians, or socialists, or some other small third party, and the largest block, 40 percent, say they're independents. So, most Americans are not partisan, and most of the people in the independent camp fall somewhere in between, so even though we have tremendous overlap between the views on these fiscal issues of Democrats and Republicans, we have even more overlap when you add in the independents. Now we get to fight about all sorts of other issues. We get to hate each other on gun control and abortion and the environment, but on these fiscal issues, these important fiscal issues, we just are not anywhere nearly as divided as people say.

And in fact, there's this other group of people who are not as divided as people might think, and that group is economists. I talk to a lot of economists, and back in the '70s and '80s it was ugly being an economist. You were in what they called the saltwater camp, meaning Harvard, Princeton, MIT, Stanford, Berkeley, or you were in the freshwater camp, University of Chicago, University of Rochester. You were a free market capitalist economist or you were a Keynesian liberal economist, and these people didn't go to each other's weddings, they snubbed each other at conferences. It's still ugly to this day, but in my experience, it is really, really hard to find an economist under 40 who still has that kind of way of seeing the world. The vast majority of economists -- it is so uncool to call yourself an ideologue of either camp. The phrase that you want, if you're a graduate student or a postdoc or you're a professor, a 38-

year-old economics professor, is, "I'm an empiricist. I go by the data." And the data is very clear. None of these major theories have been completely successful. The 20th century, the last hundred years, is riddled with disastrous examples of times that one school or the other tried to explain the past or predict the future and just did an awful, awful job, so the economics profession has acquired some degree of modesty. They still are an awfully arrogant group of people, I will assure you, but they're now arrogant about their impartiality, and they, too, see a tremendous range of potential outcomes.

And this nonpartisanship is something that exists, that has existed in secret in America for years and years and years. I've spent a lot of the fall talking to the three major organizations that survey American political attitudes: Pew Research, the University of Chicago's National Opinion Research Center, and the most important but the least known is the American National Election Studies group that is the world's longest, most respected poll of political attitudes. They've been doing it since 1948, and what they show consistently throughout is that it's almost impossible to find Americans who are consistent ideologically, who consistently support, "No we mustn't tax, and we must limit the size of government," or, "No, we must encourage government to play a larger role in redistribution and correcting the ills of capitalism." Those groups are very, very small. The vast majority of people, they pick and choose, they see compromise and they change over time when they hear a better argument or a worse argument. And that part of it has not changed. What has changed is how people respond to vague questions. If you ask people vague questions, like, "Do you think there should be more government or less government?" "Do you think government should" — especially if you use loaded language -- "Do you think the government should provide handouts?" Or, "Do you think the government should redistribute?" Then you can see radical partisan change. But when you get specific, when you actually ask about the actual taxing and spending issues under consideration, people are remarkably centrist, they're remarkably open to compromise.

So, what we have, then, when you think about the fiscal cliff, don't think of it as the American people fundamentally can't stand each other on these issues and that we must be ripped apart into two separate warring nations. Think of it as a tiny, tiny number of ancient economists and misrepresentative ideologues have captured the process. And they've captured the process through familiar ways, through a primary system which encourages that small group of people's voices, because that small group of people, the people who answer all yeses or all noes on those ideological questions, they might be small but every one of them has a blog, every one of them has been on Fox or MSNBC in the last week. Every one of them becomes a louder and louder voice, but they don't represent us. They don't represent what our views are.

And that gets me back to the dollar, and it gets me back to reminding myself that we know this experience. We know what it's like to have these people on TV, in Congress, yelling about how the end of the world is coming if we don't adopt their view completely, because it's happened about the dollar ever since there's been a dollar. We had the battle between Jefferson and Hamilton. In 1913, we had this ugly battle over the Federal Reserve, when it was created, with vicious, angry arguments over how it would be constituted, and a general agreement that the way it was constituted was the worst possible compromise, a compromise guaranteed to destroy this valuable thing, this dollar, but then everyone agreeing, okay, so long as we're on the gold standard, it should be okay. The Fed can't mess it up so badly. But then we got off the gold standard for individuals during the Depression and we got off the gold standard as a source of international currency coordination during Richard Nixon's presidency. Each of those times, we were on the verge of complete collapse. And nothing happened at all. Throughout it all, the dollar has been one of the most long-standing, stable, reasonable currencies, and we all use it every single day, no matter what the people screaming about tell us, no matter how scared we're supposed to be.

And this long-term fiscal picture that we're in right now, I think what is most maddening about it is, if Congress were simply able to show not that they agree with each other, not that they're able to come up with the best possible compromise, but that they are able to just begin the process towards compromise, we all instantly are better off. The fear is that the world is watching. The fear is that the longer we delay any solution, the more the world will look to the U.S. not as the bedrock of stability in the global economy, but as a place that can't resolve its own fights, and the longer we put that off, the more we make the world nervous, the higher interest rates are going to be, the quicker we're going to have to face a day of horrible calamity. And so just the act of compromise itself, and sustained, real compromise, would give us even more time, would allow both sides even longer to spread out the pain and reach even more compromise down the road.

So I'm in the media. I feel like my job to make this happen is to help foster the things that seem to lead to compromise, to not talk about this in those vague and scary terms that do polarize us, but to just talk about it like what it is, not an existential crisis, not some battle between two fundamentally different religious views, but a math problem, a really solvable math problem, one where we're not all going to get what we want and one where, you know, there's going to be a little pain to spread around. But the more we address it as a practical concern, the sooner we can resolve it, and the more time we have to resolve it, paradoxically.

Chapter 3
A healthy economy should be designed to thrive, not grow [3]

Have you ever watched a baby learning to crawl? Because as any parent knows, it's gripping. First, they wriggle about on the floor, usually backwards, but then they drag themselves forwards, and then they pull themselves up to stand, and we all clap. And that simple motion of forwards and upwards, it's the most basic direction of progress we humans recognize.

We tell it in our story of evolution as well, from our lolloping ancestors to Homo erectus, finally upright, to Homo sapiens, depicted, always a man, always mid-stride.

So, no wonder we so readily believe that economic progress will take this very same shape, this ever-rising line of growth. It's time to think again, to reimagine the shape of progress, because today, we have

---

[3] kate raworth: renegade economist.

economies that need to grow, whether or not they make us thrive, and what we need, especially in the richest countries, are economies that make us thrive whether or not they grow. Yes, it's a little flippant word hiding a profound shift in mindset, but I believe this is the shift we need to make if we, humanity, are going to thrive here together this century.

So, where did this obsession with growth come from? Well, GDP, gross domestic product, it's just the total cost of goods and services sold in an economy in a year. It was invented in the 1930s, but it very soon became the overriding goal of policymaking, so much so that even today, in the richest of countries, governments think that the solution to their economic problems lies in more growth.

Just how that happened is best told through the 1960 classic by W.W. Rostow. I love it so much; I have a first-edition copy. "The Stages of Economic Growth: A Non-Communist Manifesto."

You can just smell the politics, huh? And Rostow tells us that all economies need to pass through five stages of growth: first, traditional society, where a nation's output is limited by its technology, its institutions and mindset; but then the preconditions for takeoff, where we get the beginnings of a banking industry, the mechanization of work and the belief that growth is necessary for something beyond itself, like national dignity or a better life for the children; then takeoff, where compound interest is built into the economy's institutions and growth becomes the normal condition; fourth is the drive to maturity where you can have any industry you want, no matter your natural resource base; and the fifth and final stage, the age of high-mass consumption where people can buy all the consumer goods they want, like bicycles and sewing machines -- this was 1960, remember.

Well, you can hear the implicit airplane metaphor in this story, but this plane is like no other, because it can never be allowed to land. Rostow left us flying into the sunset of mass consumerism, and he knew it. As he wrote, "And then the question beyond, where history offers us only fragments. What to do when the increase in real income itself loses its charm?" He asked that question, but he never answered it, and here's why. The year was 1960, he was an advisor to the presidential candidate John F. Kennedy, who was running for election on the promise of five-percent growth, so Rostow's job was to keep that plane flying, not to ask if, how, or when it could ever be allowed to land.

So here we are, flying into the sunset of mass consumerism over half a century on, with economies that have come to expect, demand and depend upon unending growth, because we're financially, politically and socially addicted to it. We're financially addicted to growth, because today's financial system is designed to pursue the highest rate of monetary return, putting publicly traded companies under constant pressure to deliver growing sales, growing market share and growing profits, and because banks create money as debt bearing interest, which must be repaid with more. We're politically addicted to growth because politicians want to raise tax revenue without raising taxes and a growing GDP seems a sure way to do that. And no politician wants to lose their place in the G-20 family photo.

But if their economy stops growing while the rest keep going, well, they'll be booted out by the next emerging powerhouse. And we are socially addicted to growth, because thanks to a century of consumer propaganda, which fascinatingly was created by Edward Bernays, the nephew of Sigmund Freud, who realized that his uncle's psychotherapy could be turned into very lucrative retail therapy if we could be convinced to believe that we transform ourselves every time we buy something more.

None of these addictions are insurmountable, but they all deserve far more attention than they currently get, because look where this journey has been taking us. Global GDP is 10 times bigger than it was in 1950 and that increase has brought prosperity to billions of people, but the global economy has also become incredibly divisive, with the vast share of returns to wealth now accruing to a fraction of the global one percent. And the economy has become incredibly degenerative, rapidly destabilizing this delicately balanced planet on which all of our lives depend. Our politicians know it, and so they offer new destinations for growth. You can have green growth, inclusive growth, smart, resilient, balanced growth. Choose any future you want so long as you choose growth.

I think it's time to choose a higher ambition, a far bigger one, because humanity's 21st century challenge is clear: to meet the needs of all people within the means of this extraordinary, unique, living planet so that we and the rest of nature can thrive.

Progress on this goal isn't going to be measured with the metric of money. We need a dashboard of indicators. And when I sat down to try and draw a picture of what that might look like, strange though this is going to sound, it came out looking like a doughnut. I know, I'm sorry, but let me introduce you to the one doughnut that might actually turn out to be good for us. So, imagine humanity's resource use radiating out from the middle. That hole in the middle is a place where people are falling short on life's essentials. They don't have the food, health care, education, political voice, housing that every person needs for a life of dignity and opportunity. We want to get everybody out of the hole, over the social foundation and into that green doughnut itself. But, and it's a big but, we cannot let our collective resource use overshoot that outer circle, the ecological ceiling, because there we put so much pressure on this extraordinary planet that we begin to kick it out of kilter. We cause climate breakdown, we acidify the oceans, a hole in the ozone layer, pushing ourselves beyond the planetary boundaries of the life-supporting systems that have for the last 11,000 years made earth such a benevolent home to humanity.

So, this double-sided challenge to meet the needs of all within the means of the planet, it invites a new shape of progress, no longer this ever-rising line of growth, but a sweet spot for humanity, thriving in dynamic balance between the foundation and the ceiling. And I was really struck once I'd drawn this picture to realize that the symbol of well-being in many ancient cultures reflects this very same sense of dynamic balance, from the Maori Takarangi to the Taoist Yin Yang, the Buddhist endless knot, the Celtic double spiral.

So, can we find this dynamic balance in the 21st century? Well, that's a key question, because as these red wedges show, right now we are far from balanced, falling short and overshooting at the same time. Look in that hole, you can see that millions or billions of people worldwide still fall short on their most basic of needs. And yet, we've already overshot at least four of these planetary boundaries, risking irreversible impact of climate breakdown and ecosystem collapse. This is the state of humanity and our planetary home. We, the people of the early 21st century, this is our selfie.

No economist from last century saw this picture, so why would we imagine that their theories would be up for taking on its challenges? We need ideas of our own, because we are the first generation to see this and probably the last with a real chance of turning this story around. You see, 20th century economics assured us that if growth creates inequality, don't try to redistribute, because more growth will even things up again. If growth creates pollution, don't try to regulate, because more growth will clean things up again.

Except, it turns out, it doesn't, and it won't. We need to create economies that tackle this shortfall and overshoot together, by design. We need economies that are regenerative and distributive by design. You see, we've inherited degenerative industries. We take earth's materials, make them into stuff we want, use it for a while, often only once, and then throw it away, and that is pushing us over planetary boundaries, so we need to bend those arrows around, create economies that work with and within the cycles of the living world, so that resources are never used up but used again and again, economies that run on sunlight, where waste from one process is food for the next.

And this kind of regenerative design is popping up everywhere. Over a hundred cities worldwide, from Quito to Oslo, from Harare to Hobart, already generate more than 70 percent of their electricity from sun, wind and waves. Cities like London, Glasgow, Amsterdam are pioneering circular city design, finding ways to turn the waste from one urban process into food for the next. And from Tigray, Ethiopia to Queensland, Australia, farmers and foresters are regenerating once-barren landscapes so that it teems with life again.

But as well as being regenerative by design, our economies must be distributive by design, and we've got unprecedented opportunities for making that happen, because 20th-century centralized technologies, institutions, concentrated wealth, knowledge and power in few hands. This century, we can design our technologies and institutions to distribute wealth, knowledge and empowerment to many. Instead of fossil fuel energy and large-scale manufacturing, we've got renewable energy networks, digital platforms and 3D printing. 200 years of corporate control of intellectual property is being upended by the bottom-up, open-source, peer-to-peer knowledge commons. And corporations that still pursue maximum rate of return for their shareholders, well they suddenly look rather out of date next to social enterprises that are designed to generate multiple forms of value and share it with those throughout their networks. If we can harness today's technologies, from AI to blockchain to the Internet of Things to material science, if we can harness these in service of distributive design, we can ensure that health care, education, finance, energy, political voice reaches and empowers those people who need it most. You see, regenerative and distributive design create extraordinary opportunities for the 21st-century economy.

So, where does this leave Rostow's airplane ride? Well, for some it still carries the hope of endless green growth, the idea that thanks to dematerialization, exponential GDP growth can go on forever while resource use keeps falling. But look at the data. This is a flight of fancy. Yes, we need to dematerialize our economies, but this dependency on unending growth cannot be decoupled from resource use on anything like the scale required to bring us safely back within planetary boundaries.

I know this way of thinking about growth is unfamiliar, because growth is good, no? We want our children to grow, our gardens to grow. Yes, look to nature and growth is a wonderful, healthy source of life. It's a phase, but many economies like Ethiopia and Nepal today may be in that phase. Their economies are growing at seven percent a year. But look again to nature, because from your children's feet to the Amazon forest, nothing in nature grows forever. Things grow, and they grow up and they mature, and it's only by doing so that they can thrive for a very long time. We already know this. If I told you my friend went to the doctor who told her she had a growth that feels very different, because we intuitively understand that when something tries to grow forever within a healthy, living, thriving system, it's a threat to the health of the whole. So why would we imagine that our economies would be the one system that could buck this trend and succeed by growing forever? We urgently need financial, political and social innovations that enable us to overcome this structural dependency on growth, so that we can instead focus on thriving and balance within the social and the ecological boundaries of the doughnut.

And if the mere idea of boundaries makes you feel, well, bounded, think again. Because the world's most ingenious people turn boundaries into the source of their creativity. From Mozart on his five-octave piano Jimi Hendrix on his six-string guitar, Serena Williams on a tennis court, it's boundaries that unleash our potential. And the doughnut's boundaries unleash the potential for humanity to thrive with boundless creativity, participation, belonging and meaning.

It's going to take all the ingenuity that we have got to get there, so bring it on.

Chapter 4
The hidden force in global economics: sending money home [4]

There are millions of people who migrate each year. With the help of the family, they cross oceans, they cross deserts, they cross rivers, they cross mountains. They risk their lives to realize a dream, and that dream is as simple as having a decent job somewhere so they can send money home and help the family, which has helped them before.

There are 232 million international migrants in the world. These are people who live in a country other than their country of birth. If there was a country made up of only international migrants, that would be larger, in population, than Brazil. That would be larger, in its size of the economy, than France. Some 180 million of them, from poor countries, send money home regularly.

)[4] Suhas Ketkar, Dilip Ratha: Innovative Financing for Development, amazon, 2008.

Those sums of money are called remittances. Here is a fact that might surprise you: 413 billion dollars, 413 billion dollars was the amount of remittances sent last year by migrants to developing countries. Migrants from developing countries, money sent to developing countries — 413 billion dollars. That's a remarkable number because that is three times the size of the total of development aid money. And yet, you and I, my colleagues in Washington, we endlessly debate and discuss about development aid, while we ignore remittances as small change.

True, people send 200 dollars per month, on average. But, repeated month after month, by millions of people, these sums of money add up to rivers of foreign currency. So, India, last year, received 72 billion dollars, larger than its IT exports. In Egypt remittances are three times the size of revenues from the Suez Canal. In Tajikistan, remittances are 42 percent of GDP. And in poorer countries, smaller countries, fragile countries, conflict-afflicted countries, remittances are a lifeline, as in Somalia or in Haiti.

No wonder these flows have huge impacts on economies and on poor people. Remittances, unlike private investment money, they don't flow back at the first sign of trouble in the country. They actually act like an insurance. When the family is in trouble, facing hardship, facing hard times, remittances increase, they act like an insurance. Migrants send more money then. Unlike development aid money, that must go through official agencies, through governments, remittances directly reach the poor, reach the family, and often with business advice.

So, in Nepal, the share of poor people was 42 percent in 1995, the share of poor people in the population. By 2005, a decade later, at a time of political crisis, economic crisis, the share of poor people went down to 31 percent. That decline in poverty, most of it, about half of it, is believed to be because of remittances from India, another poor country. In El Salvador, the school dropout rate among children is lower in families that receive remittances. In Mexico and Sri Lanka, the birth weight of children is higher among families that receive remittances.

Remittances are dollars wrapped with care. Migrants send money home for food, for buying necessities, for building houses, for funding education, for funding healthcare for the elderly, for business investments for friends and family. Migrants send even more money home for special occasions like a surgery or a wedding. And migrants also send money, perhaps far too many times, for unexpected funerals that they cannot attend.

Much as these flows do all that good, there are barriers to these flows of remittances, these 400 billion dollars of remittances. Foremost among them is the exorbitant cost of sending money home. Money transfer companies structure their fees to milk the poor. They will say, "Up to 500 dollars if you want to send, we will charge you 30 dollars fixed." If you are poor and if you have only 200 dollars to send, you have to pay that $30 fee. The global average cost of sending money is eight percent. That means you send 100 dollars, the family on the other side receives only 92 dollars. To send money to Africa, the cost is even higher: 12 percent. To send money within Africa, the cost is even higher: over 20 percent. For example, sending money from Benin to Nigeria. And then there is the case of Venezuela, where, because of exchange controls, you send 100 dollars and you are lucky if the family on the other side receives even 10 dollars. Of course, nobody sends money to Venezuela through the official channel. It all goes in suitcases. Where ever costs are high, money goes underground.

And what is worse, many developing countries actually have a blanket ban on sending money out of the country. Many rich nations also have a blanket ban on sending money to specific countries. So, is it that there are no options, no better options, cheaper options, to send money?

There are. M-Pesa in Kenya enables people to send money and receive money at a fixed cost of only 60 cents per transaction. U.S. Fed started a program with Mexico to enable money service businesses to send money to Mexico for a fixed cost of only 67 cents per transaction. And yet, these faster, cheaper, better options can't be applied internationally because of the fear of money laundering, even though there is little data to support any connection, any significant connection between money laundering and these small remittance transactions. Many international banks now are wary of hosting bank accounts of money service businesses, especially those serving Somalia.

Somalia, a country where the per capita income is only 250 dollars per year. Monthly remittances, on average, to Somalia is larger than that amount. Remittances are the lifeblood of Somalia. And yet, this is an example of the right hand giving a lot of aid, while the left hand is cutting the lifeblood to that economy, through regulations. Then there is the case of poor people from villages, like me. In the villages, the only place where you can get money is through the post office. Most of the governments in the world have allowed their post offices to have exclusive partnerships with money transfer companies. So, if I have to send money to my father in the village, I must send money through that particular money transfer company, even if the cost is high. I cannot go to a cheaper option. This has to go.

So, what can international organizations and social entrepreneurs do to reduce the cost of sending money home? First, relax regulations on small remittances under 1,000 dollars. Governments should recognize that small remittances are not money laundering. Second, governments should abolish exclusive partnerships between their post office and the money transfer company. For that matter, between the post office and any national banking system that has a large network that serves the poor. In fact, they should promote competition, open up the partnership so that we will bring down costs like we did, like they did, in the telecommunications industry. You have seen what has happened there. Third, large nonprofit philanthropic organizations should create a remittance platform on a nonprofit basis. They should create a nonprofit remittance platform to serve the money transfer companies so that they can send money at a low cost, while complying with all the complex regulations all over the world.

The development community should set a goal of reducing remittance costs to one percent from the current eight percent. If we reduce costs to one percent, that would release a saving of 30 billion dollars per year. Thirty billion dollars, that's larger than the entire bilateral aid budget going to Africa per year. That is larger than, or almost similar to, the total aid budget of the United States government, the largest donor on the planet. Actually, the savings would be larger than that 30 billion because remittance channels are also used for aid, trade and investment purposes.

Another major impediment to the flow of remittances reaching the family is the large and exorbitant and illegal cost of recruitment, fees that migrants pay, migrant workers pay to laborers who found them the job.

I was in Dubai a few years ago. I visited a camp for workers. It was 8 in the evening, dark, hot, humid. Workers were coming back from their grueling day of work, and I struck a conversation with a Bangladeshi construction worker. He was preoccupied that he is sending money home, he has been sending money home for a few months now, and the money is mostly going to the recruitment agent, to the labor agent who found him that job. And in my mind, I could picture the wife waiting for the monthly remittance. The remittance arrives. She takes the money and hands it over to the recruitment agent, while the children are looking on. This has to stop.

It is not only construction workers from Bangladesh, it is all the workers. There are millions of migrant workers who suffer from this problem. A construction worker from Bangladesh, on an average, pays about 4,000 dollars in recruitment fees for a job that gives him only 2,000 dollars per year in income. That means that for the two years or three years of his life, he is basically sending money to pay for the recruitment fees. The family doesn't get to see any of it.

It is not only Dubai; it is the dark underbelly of every major city in the world. It is not only Bangladeshi construction workers; it is workers from all over the world. It is not only men. Women are especially vulnerable to recruitment malpractices.

One of the most exciting and newest things happening in the area of remittances is how to mobilize, through innovation, diaspora saving and diaspora giving. Migrants send money home, but they also save a large amount of money where they live. Annually, migrant savings are estimated to be 500 billion dollars. Most of that money is parked in bank deposits that give you zero percent interest rate. If a country were to come and offer a three percent or four percent interest rate, and then say that the money would be used for building schools, roads, airports, train systems in the country of origin, a lot of migrants would be interested in parting with their money because it's not only financial gains that give them an opportunity to stay engaged with their country's development. Remittance channels can be used to sell these bonds to migrants because when they come on a monthly basis to send remittances, that's when you can actually sell it to them. You can also do the same for mobilizing diaspora giving. I would love to invest in a bullet train system in India and I would love to contribute to efforts to fight malaria in my village. Remittances are a great way of sharing prosperity between places in a targeted way that benefits those who need them most.

Remittances empower people. We must do all we can to make remittances and recruitment safer and cheaper. And it can be done.

As for myself, I have been away from India for two decades now. My wife is a Venezuelan. My children are

Americans. Increasingly, I feel like a global citizen. And yet, I am growing nostalgic about my country of birth. I want to be in India and in the U.S. at the same time. My parents are not there anymore. My brothers and sisters have moved on. There is no real urgency for me to send money home. And yet, from time to time, I send money home to friends, to relatives, to the village, to be there, to stay engaged — that's part of my identity. And, I'm still striving to be a poet for the hardworking migrants and their struggle to break free of the cycle of poverty.

Chapter 5
The rise of the new global super-rich [5]

We are living in an age of surging income inequality, particularly between those at the very top and everyone else. This shift is the most striking in the U.S. and in the U.K., but it's a global phenomenon. It's happening in communist China, in formerly communist Russia, it's happening in India, in my own native Canada. We're even seeing it in cozy social democracies like Sweden, Finland and Germany.

Let me give you a few numbers to place what's happening. In the 1970s, the One Percent accounted for about 10 percent of the national income in the United States. Today, their share has more than doubled to above 20 percent. But what's even more striking is what's happening at the very tippy top of the income distribution. The 0.1 percent in the U.S. today account for more than eight percent of the

---

)[5] Chrystia Freeland: plutocracy chronicle.

national income. They are where the One Percent was 30 years ago. Let me give you another number to put that in perspective, and this is a figure that was calculated in 2005 by Robert Reich, the Secretary of Labor in the Clinton administration. Reich took the wealth of two admittedly very rich men, Bill Gates and Warren Buffett, and he found that it was equivalent to the wealth of the bottom 40 percent of the U.S. population, 120 million people. Now, as it happens, Warren Buffett is not only himself a plutocrat, he is one of the most astute observers of that phenomenon, and he has his own favorite number. Buffett likes to point out that in 1992, the combined wealth of the people on the Forbes 400 list -- and this is the list of the 400 richest Americans -- was 300 billion dollars. Just think about it. You didn't even need to be a billionaire to get on that list in 1992. Well, today, that figure has more than quintupled to 1.7 trillion, and I probably don't need to tell you that we haven't seen anything similar happen to the middle class, whose wealth has stagnated if not actually decreased.

So, we're living in the age of the global plutocracy, but we've been slow to notice it. One of the reasons, I think, is a sort of boiled frog phenomenon. Changes which are slow and gradual can be hard to notice even if their ultimate impact is quite dramatic. Think about what happened, after all, to the poor frog. But I think there's something else going on. Talking about income inequality, even if you're not on the Forbes 400 list, can make us feel uncomfortable. It feels less positive, less optimistic, to talk about how the pie is sliced than to think about how to make the pie bigger. And if you do happen to be on the Forbes 400 list, talking about income distribution, and inevitably its cousin, income redistribution, can be downright threatening.

So, we're living in the age of surging income inequality, especially at the top. What's driving it, and what can we do about it?

One set of causes is political: lower taxes, deregulation, particularly of financial services, privatization, weaker legal protections for trade unions, all of these have contributed to more and more income going to the very, very top.

A lot of these political factors can be broadly lumped under the category of "crony capitalism," political changes that benefit a group of well-connected insiders but don't actually do much good for the rest of us. In practice, getting rid of crony capitalism is incredibly difficult. Think of all the years reformers of various stripes have tried to get rid of corruption in Russia, for instance, or how hard it is to re-regulate the banks even after the most profound financial crisis since the Great Depression, or even how difficult it is to get the big multinational companies, including those whose motto might be "don't do evil," to pay taxes at a rate even approaching that paid by the middle class. But while getting rid of crony capitalism in practice is really, really hard, at least intellectually, it's an easy problem. After all, no one is actually in favor of crony capitalism. Indeed, this is one of those rare issues that unites the left and the right. A critique of crony capitalism is as central to the Tea Party as it is to Occupy Wall Street.

But if crony capitalism is, intellectually at least, the easy part of the problem, things get trickier when you look at the economic drivers of surging income inequality. In and of themselves, these aren't too mysterious. Globalization and the technology revolution, the twin economic transformations which are changing our lives and transforming the global economy, are also powering the rise of the super-rich. Just think about it. For the first time in history, if you are an energetic entrepreneur with a brilliant new idea or a fantastic new product, you have almost instant, almost frictionless access to a global market of more than a billion people. As a result, if you are very, very smart and very, very lucky, you can get very, very rich very, very quickly. The latest poster boy for this phenomenon is David Karp. The 26-year-old founder of Tumblr recently sold his company to Yahoo for 1.1 billion dollars. Think about that for a minute: 1.1 billion dollars, 26 years old. It's easiest to see how the technology revolution and globalization are creating this sort of superstar effect in highly visible fields, like sports and entertainment. We can all watch how a fantastic athlete or a fantastic performer can today leverage his or her skills across the global economy as never before. But today, that superstar effect is happening across the entire economy. We have superstar technologists. We have superstar bankers. We have superstar lawyers and superstar architects. There are superstar cooks and superstar farmers. There are even, and this is my personal favorite example, superstar dentists, the most dazzling exemplar of whom is Bernard Touati, the Frenchman who ministers to the smiles of fellow superstars like Russian oligarch Roman Abramovich or European-born American fashion designer Diane von Furstenberg.

But while it's pretty easy to see how globalization and the technology revolution are creating this global plutocracy, what's a lot harder is figuring out what to think about it. And that's because, in contrast with crony capitalism, so much of what globalization and the technology revolution have done is highly positive. Let's start with technology. I love the Internet. I love my mobile devices. I love the fact that they mean that whoever chooses to will be able to watch this talk far beyond this auditorium. I'm even more of a fan of globalization. This is the transformation which has lifted hundreds of millions of the world's poorest people out of poverty and into the middle class, and if you happen to live in the rich part of the world, it's made many new products affordable -- who do you think built your iPhone? — and things that we've relied on for a long time much cheaper. Think of your dishwasher or your t-shirt.

So, what's not to like? Well, a few things. One of the things that worries me is how easily what you might call meritocratic plutocracy can become crony plutocracy. Imagine you're a brilliant entrepreneur who has successfully sold that idea or that product to the global billions and become a billionaire in the process. It gets tempting at that point to use your economic nous to manipulate the rules of the global political economy in your own favor. And that's no mere hypothetical example. Think about Amazon, Apple, Google, Starbucks. These are among the world's most admired, most beloved, most innovative companies. They also happen to be particularly adept at working the international tax system so as to lower their tax bill very, very significantly. And why stop at just playing the global political and economic system as it exists to your own maximum advantage? Once you have the tremendous economic power that we're seeing at the very, very top of the income distribution and the political power that inevitably entails, it becomes tempting as well to start trying to change the rules of the game in your own favor. Again, this is no mere hypothetical. It's what the Russian oligarchs did in creating the sale-of-the-century privatization of Russia's natural resources. It's one way of describing what happened with deregulation of the financial services in the U.S. and the U.K.

A second thing that worries me is how easily meritocratic plutocracy can become aristocracy. One way of describing the plutocrats is as alpha geeks, and they are people who are acutely aware of how important highly sophisticated analytical and quantitative skills are in today's economy. That's why they are spending unprecedented time and resources educating their own children. The middle class is spending more on schooling too, but in the global educational arms race that starts at nursery school and ends at Harvard, Stanford or MIT, the 99 percent is increasingly outgunned by the One Percent. The result is something that economists Alan Krueger and Miles Corak call the Great Gatsby Curve. As income inequality increases, social mobility decreases. The plutocracy may be a meritocracy, but increasingly you have to be born on the top rung of the ladder to even take part in that race.

The third thing, and this is what worries me the most, is the extent to which those same largely positive forces which are driving the rise of the global plutocracy also happen to be hollowing out the middle class in Western industrialized economies. Let's start with technology. Those same forces that are creating billionaires are also devouring many traditional middle-class jobs. When's the last time you used a travel agent? And in contrast with the industrial revolution, the titans of our new economy aren't creating that many new jobs. At its zenith, G.M. employed hundreds of thousands, Facebook fewer than 10,000. The same is true of globalization. For all that it is raising hundreds of millions of people out of poverty in the emerging markets, it's also outsourcing a lot of jobs from the developed Western economies. The terrifying reality is that there is no economic rule which automatically translates increased economic growth into widely shared prosperity. That's shown in what I consider to be the scariest economic statistic of our time. Since the late 1990s, increases in productivity have been decoupled from increases in wages and employment. That means that our countries are getting richer, our companies are getting more efficient, but we're not creating more jobs and we're not paying people, as a whole, more.

One scary conclusion you could draw from all of this is to worry about structural unemployment. What worries me more is a different nightmare scenario. After all, in a totally free labor market, we could find jobs for pretty much everyone. The dystopia that worries me is a universe in which a few geniuses invent Google and its ilk and the rest of us are employed giving them massages.

So, when I get really depressed about all of this, I comfort myself in thinking about the Industrial Revolution. After all, for all its grim, satanic mills, it worked out pretty well, didn't it? After all, all of us here are richer, healthier, taller -- well, there are a few exceptions — and live longer than our ancestors in the early 19th century. But it's important to remember that before we learned how to share the fruits of the Industrial Revolution with the broad swathes of society, we had to go through two depressions, the Great Depression of the 1930s, the Long Depression of the 1870s, two world wars, communist revolutions in Russia and in China, and an era of tremendous social and political upheaval in the West. We also, not coincidentally, went through an era of tremendous social and political inventions. We created the modern welfare state. We created public education. We created public health care. We created public pensions. We created unions.

Today, we are living through an era of economic transformation comparable in its scale and its scope to the Industrial Revolution. To be sure that this new economy benefits us all and not just the plutocrats, we need to embark on an era of comparably ambitious social and political change. We need a new Deal.

Chapter 6
Government - investor, risk-taker, innovator [6]

Have you ever asked yourselves why it is that companies, the really cool companies, the innovative ones, the creative, new economy-type companies -- Apple, Google, Facebook -- are coming out of one particular country, the United States of America? Usually when I say this, someone says, "Spotify! That's Europe." But, yeah. It has not had the impact that these other companies have had.

Now what I do is I'm an economist, and I actually study the relationship between innovation and economic growth at the level of the company, the industry and the nation, and I work with policymakers worldwide, especially in the European Commission, but recently also in interesting places like China, and I can tell you that that question is on the tip of all of their tongues: Where are the European

---

[6] Mariana Mazzucato: The Value of Everything: Making and Taking in the Global Economy 2nd Edition, penguin, 2019.

Googles? What is the secret behind the Silicon Valley growth model, which they understand is different from this old economy growth model? And what is interesting is that often, even if we're in the 21st century, we kind of come down in the end to these ideas of market versus state. It's talked about in these modern ways, but the idea is that somehow, behind places like Silicon Valley, the secret have been different types of market-making mechanisms, the private initiative, whether this be about a dynamic venture capital sector that's actually able to provide that high-risk finance to these innovative companies, the gazelles as we often call them, which traditional banks are scared of, or different types of really successful commercialization policies which actually allow these companies to bring these great inventions, their products, to the market and actually get over this really scary Death Valley period in which many companies instead fail.

But what really interests me, especially nowadays and because of what's happening politically around the world, is the language that's used, the narrative, the discourse, the images, the actual words. So, we often are presented with the kind of words like that the private sector is also much more innovative because it's able to think out of the box. They are more dynamic. Think of Steve Jobs' really inspirational speech to the 2005 graduating class at Stanford, where he said to be innovative, you've got to stay hungry, stay foolish. Right? So, these guys are kind of the hungry and foolish and colorful guys, right? And in places like Europe, it might be more equitable, we might even be a bit better dressed and eat better than the U.S., but the problem is this damn public sector. It's a bit too big, and it hasn't actually allowed these things like dynamic venture capital and commercialization to actually be able to really be as fruitful as it could. And even really respectable newspapers, some that I'm actually subscribed to, the words they use are, you know, the state as this Leviathan. Right? This monster with big tentacles. They're very explicit in these editorials. They say, "You know, the state, it's necessary to fix these little market failures when you have public goods or different types of negative externalities like pollution, but you know what, what is the next big revolution going to be after the Internet? We all hope it might be something green, or all of this nanotech stuff, and in order for that stuff to happen," they say -- this was a special issue on the next industrial revolution -- they say, "the state, just stick to the basics, right? Fund the infrastructure. Fund the schools. Even fund the basic research, because this is popularly recognized, in fact, as a big public good which private companies don't want to invest in, do that, but you know what? Leave the rest to the revolutionaries." Those colorful, out-of-the-box kinds of thinkers. They're often called garage tinkerers, because some of them actually did some things in garages, even though that's partly a myth. And so, what I want to do with you in, oh God, only 10 minutes, is to really think again this juxtaposition, because it actually has massive, massive implications beyond innovation policy, which just happens to be the area that I often talk with policymakers. It has huge implications, even with this whole notion that we have on where, when and why we should actually be cutting back on public spending and different types of public services which, of course, as we know, are increasingly being outsourced because of this juxtaposition. Right? I mean, the reason that we need to maybe have free schools or charter schools is in order to make them more innovative without being emburdened by this heavy hand of the state curriculum, or something. So, these kinds of words are constantly, these juxtapositions come up everywhere, not just with innovation policy.

And so, to think again, there's no reason that you should believe me, so just think of some of the smartest revolutionary things that you have in your pockets and do not turn it on, but you might want to take it out, your iPhone. Ask who actually funded the really cool, revolutionary thinking-out-of-the-box things in the iPhone. What actually makes your phone a smartphone, basically, instead of a stupid phone? So, the Internet, which you can surf the web anywhere you are in the world; GPS, where you can actually know where you are anywhere in the world; the touchscreen display, which makes it also a really easy-to-use phone for anybody. These are the very smart, revolutionary bits about the iPhone, and they're all government-funded. And the point is that the Internet was funded by DARPA, U.S. Department of Defense. GPS was funded by the military's Navstar program. Even Siri was actually funded by DARPA. The touchscreen display was funded by two public grants by the CIA and the NSF to two public university researchers at the University of Delaware. Now, you might be thinking, "Well, she's just said the word 'defense' and 'military' an awful lot," but what's really interesting is that this is actually true in sector after sector and department after department. So the pharmaceutical industry, which I am personally very interested in because I've actually had the fortune to study it in quite some depth, is wonderful to be asking this question about the revolutionary versus non-revolutionary bits, because each and every medicine can actually be divided up on whether it really is revolutionary or incremental. So the new molecular entities with priority rating are the revolutionary new drugs, whereas the slight variations of existing drugs -- Viagra, different color, different dosage -- are the less revolutionary ones. And it turns out that a full 75 percent of the new molecular entities with priority rating are actually funded in boring,

Kafka-ian public sector labs. This doesn't mean that Big Pharma is not spending on innovation. They do. They spend on the marketing part. They spend on the D part of R&D. They spend an awful lot on buying back their stock, which is quite problematic. In fact, companies like Pfizer and Amgen recently have spent more money in buying back their shares to boost their stock price than on R&D.

Now, what's interesting in all of this is the state, in all these examples, was doing so much more than just fixing market failures. It was actually shaping and creating markets. It was funding not only the basic research, which again is a typical public good, but even the applied research. It was even, God forbid, being a venture capitalist. So, these SBIR and SDTR programs, which give small companies early-stage finance have not only been extremely important compared to private venture capital, but also have become increasingly important. Why? Because, as many of us know, V.C. is actually quite short-term. They want their returns in three to five years. Innovation takes a much longer time than that, 15 to 20 years. And so, this whole notion -- I mean, this is the point, right? Who's actually funding the hard stuff? Of course, it's not just the state. The private sector does a lot. But the narrative that we've always been told is the state is important for the basics, but not really providing that sort of high-risk, revolutionary thinking out of the box. In all these sectors, from funding the Internet to doing the spending, but also the envisioning, the strategic vision, for these investments, it was actually coming within the state. The nanotechnology sector is actually fascinating to study this, because the word itself, nanotechnology, came from within government.

And so, there's huge implications of this. First of all, of course I'm not someone, this old-fashioned person, market versus state. What we all know in dynamic capitalism is that what we actually need are public-private partnerships. But the point is, by constantly depicting the state part as necessary but actually -- a bit boring and often a bit dangerous kind of Leviathan, I think we've actually really stunted the possibility to build these public-private partnerships in a really dynamic way. Even the words that we often use to justify the "P" part, the public part -- well, they're both P's -- with public-private partnerships is in terms of de-risking. What the public sector did in all these examples I just gave you, and there's many more, which myself and other colleagues have been looking at, is doing much more than de-risking. It's kind of been taking on that risk. Bring it on. It's actually been the one thinking out of the box. But also, I'm sure you all have had experience with local, regional, national governments, and your kind of like, "You know what, that Kafka-ian bureaucrat, I've met him." That whole juxtaposition thing, it's kind of there. Well, there's a self-fulfilling prophecy. By talking about the state as kind of irrelevant, boring, it's sometimes that we actually create those organizations in that way. So, what we have to actually do is build these entrepreneurial state organizations. DARPA, that funded the Internet and Siri, actually thought really hard about this, how to welcome failure, because you will fail. You will fail when you innovative. One out of 10 experiments have any success. And the V.C. guys know this, and they're able to actually fund the other losses from that one success.

And this brings me, actually, probably, to the biggest implication, and this has huge implications beyond innovation. If the state is more than just a market fixer, if it actually is a market shaper, and in doing that has had to take on this massive risk, what happened to the reward? We all know, if you've ever taken a finance course, the first thing you're taught is sort of the risk-reward relationship, and so some people are foolish enough or probably smart enough if they have time to wait, to actually invest in stocks, because they're higher risk which over time will make a greater reward than bonds, that whole risk-reward thing. Well, where's the reward for the state of having taken on these massive risks and actually been foolish enough to have done the Internet? The Internet was crazy. It really was. I mean, the probability of failure was massive. You had to be completely nuts to do it, and luckily, they were. Now, we don't even get to this question about rewards unless you actually depict the state as this risk-taker. And the problem is that economists often think, well, there is a reward back to the state. It's tax. You know, the companies will pay tax, the jobs they create will create growth so people who get those jobs and their incomes rise will come back to the state through the tax mechanism. Well, unfortunately, that's not true. Okay, it's not true because many of the jobs that are created go abroad. Globalization, and that's fine. We shouldn't be nationalistic. Let the jobs go where they have to go, perhaps. I mean, one can take a position on that. But also, these companies that have actually had this massive benefit from the state -- Apple's a great example. They even got the first -- well, not the first, but 500,000 dollars actually went to Apple, the company, through this SBIC program, which predated the SBIR program, as well as, as I said before, all the technologies behind the iPhone. And yet we know they legally, as many other companies, pay very little tax back.

So, what we really need to actually rethink is should there perhaps be a return-generating mechanism that's much more direct than tax. Why not? It could happen perhaps through equity. This, by the way, in the countries that are actually thinking about this strategically, countries like Finland in

Scandinavia, but also in China and Brazil, they're retaining equity in these investments. Sitra funded Nokia, kept equity, made a lot of money, it's a public funding agency in Finland, which then funded the next round of Nokias. The Brazilian Development Bank, which is providing huge amounts of funds today to clean technology, they just announced a $56 billion program for the future on this, is retaining equity in these investments. So to put it provocatively, had the U.S. government thought about this, and maybe just brought back just something called an innovation fund, you can bet that, you know, if even just .05 percent of the profits from what the Internet produced had come back to that innovation fund, there would be so much more money to spend today on green technology. Instead, many of the state budgets which in theory are trying to do that are being constrained. But perhaps even more important, we heard before about the one percent, the 99 percent. If the state is thought about in this more strategic way, as one of the lead players in the value creation mechanism, because that's what we're talking about, right? Who are the different players in creating value in the economy, and is the state's role, has it been sort of dismissed as being a backseat player? If we can actually have a broader theory of value creation and allow us to actually admit what the state has been doing and reap something back, it might just be that in the next round, and I hope that we all hope that the next big revolution will in fact be green, that that period of growth will not only be smart, innovation-led, not only green, but also more inclusive, so that the public schools in places like Silicon Valley can actually also benefit from that growth, because they have not.

Chapter 7
New thoughts on capital [7]

I've been working on the history of income and wealth distribution for the past 15 years, and one of the interesting lessons coming from this historical evidence is indeed that, in the long run, there is a tendency for the rate of return of capital to exceed the economy's growth rate, and this tends to lead to high concentration of wealth. Not infinite concentration of wealth, but the higher the gap between r and g, the higher the level of inequality of wealth towards which society tends to converge.

So this is a key force that I'm going to talk about today, but let me say right away that this is not the only important force in the dynamics of income and wealth distribution, and there are many other forces that play an important role in the long-run

---

)[7] Thomas Piketty: Capital in the Twenty First Century, amazon, 2014

dynamics of income and wealth distribution. Also, there is a lot of data that still needs to be collected. We know a little bit more today than we used to know, but we still know too little, and certainly there are many different processes — economic, social, political — that need to be studied more. And so, I'm going to focus today on this simple force, but that doesn't mean that other important forces do not exist.

So, most of the data I'm going to present comes from this database that's available online: the World Top Incomes Database. So this is the largest existing historical database on inequality, and this comes from the effort of over 30 scholars from several dozen countries. So let me show you a couple of facts coming from this database, and then we'll return to r bigger than g. So, fact number one is that there has been a big reversal in the ordering of income inequality between the United States and Europe over the past century. So back in 1900,

1910, income inequality was actually much higher in Europe than in the United States, whereas today, it is a lot higher in the United States. So, let me be very clear: The main explanation for this is not r bigger than g. It has more to do with changing supply and demand for skill, the race between education and technology, globalization, probably more unequal access to skills in the U.S., where you have very good, very top universities but where the bottom part of the educational system is not as good, so very unequal access to skills, and also an unprecedented rise of top managerial compensation of the United States, which is difficult to account for just on the basis of education. So, there is more going on here, but I'm not going to talk too much about this today, because I want to focus on wealth inequality.

the income inequality was between 45 and 50 percent in Europe and a little bit above 40 percent in the U.S., so there was more inequality in Europe. Then there was a sharp decline during the first half of the 20th century, and in the recent decade, you can see that the U.S. has become more unequal than Europe, and this is the first fact I just talked about. Now, the second fact is more about wealth inequality, and here the central fact is that wealth inequality is always a lot higher than income inequality, and also that wealth inequality, although it has also increased in recent decades, is still less extreme today than what it was a century ago, although the total quantity of wealth relative to income has now recovered from the very large shocks caused by World War I, the Great Depression, World War II.

On the other hand, wealth concentration was higher in Europe than in the U.S. a century ago, and now it is the opposite. But you can also show two things: First, the general level of wealth inequality is always higher than income inequality. So, remember, for income inequality, the share going to the top 10 percent was between 30 and 50 percent of total income, whereas for wealth, the share is always between 60 and 90 percent. Okay, so that's fact number one, and that's very important for what follows. Wealth concentration is always a lot higher than income concentration.

Fact number two is that the rise in wealth inequality in recent decades is still not enough to get us back to 1910. So, the big difference today, wealth inequality is still very large, with 60, 70 percent of total wealth for the top 10, but the good news is that it's actually better than one century ago, where you had 90 percent in Europe going to the top 10. So today what you have is what I call the middle 40 percent, the people who are not in the top 10 and who are not in the bottom 50, and what you can view as the wealth middle class that owns 20 to 30 percent of total wealth, national wealth, whereas they used to be poor, a century ago, when there was basically no wealth middle class. So, this is an important change, and it's interesting to see that wealth inequality has not fully recovered to pre-World War I levels, although the total quantity of wealth has recovered. Okay? So, this is the total value of wealth relative to income, and you can see that in particular in Europe, we are almost back to the pre-World War I level. So, there are really two different parts of the story here. One has to do with the total quantity of wealth that we accumulate, and there is nothing bad per se, of course, in accumulating a lot of wealth, and in particular if it is more diffuse and less concentrated. So, what we really want to focus on is the long-run evolution of wealth inequality, and what's going to happen in the future. How can we account for the fact that until World War I, wealth inequality was so high and, if anything, was rising to even higher levels, and how can we think about the future?

So, let me come to some of the explanations and speculations about the future. Let me first say that probably the best model to explain why wealth is so much more concentrated than income is a dynamic, dynastic model where individuals have a long horizon and accumulate wealth for all sorts of reasons. If people were accumulating wealth only for life cycle reasons, you know, to be able to consume when they are old, then the level of wealth inequality should be more or less in line with the level of income inequality. But it will be very difficult to explain why you have so much more wealth inequality than income inequality with a pure life cycle model, so you need a story where people also care about wealth accumulation for other reasons. So typically, they want to transmit wealth to the next generation, to their children, or sometimes they want to accumulate wealth because of the prestige, the power that goes with wealth. So there must be other reasons for accumulating wealth than just life cycle to explain what we see in the data. Now, in a large class of dynamic models of wealth accumulation with such dynastic motive for accumulating wealth, you will have all sorts of random, multiplicative shocks. So, for instance, some families have a very large number of children, so the wealth will be divided. Some families have fewer children. You also have shocks to rates of return. Some families make huge capital gains. Some made bad investments. So, you will always have some mobility in the wealth process. Some people will move up, some people will move down. The important point is that, in any such model, for a given variance of such shocks, the equilibrium level of wealth inequality will be a steeply rising function of r minus g. And intuitively, the reason why the difference between the rate of return to wealth and the growth rate is important is that initial wealth inequalities will be amplified at a faster pace with a bigger r minus g. So, take a simple example, with r equals five percent and g equals one percent, wealth holders only need to reinvest one fifth of their capital income to ensure that their wealth rises as fast as the size of the economy. So, this makes it easier to build and perpetuate large fortunes because you can consume four fifths, assuming zero tax, and you can just reinvest one fifth. So of course, some families will consume more than that, some will consume less, so there will be some mobility in the distribution, but on average, they only need to reinvest one fifth, so this allows high wealth inequalities to be sustained.

Now, you should not be surprised by the statement that r can be bigger than g forever, because, in fact, this is what happened during most of the history of mankind. And this was in a way very obvious to everybody for a simple reason, which is that growth was close to zero percent during most of the history of mankind. Growth was maybe 0.1, 0.2, 0.3 percent, but very slow growth of population and output per capita, whereas the rate of return on capital of course was not zero percent. It was, for land assets, which was the traditional form of assets in preindustrial societies, it was typically five percent. Any reader of Jane Austen would know that. If you want an annual income of 1,000 pounds, you should have a capital value of 20,000 pounds so that five percent of 20,000 is 1,000. And in a way, this was the very foundation of society, because r bigger than g was what allowed holders of wealth and assets to live off their capital income and to do something else in life than just to care about their own survival.

Now, one important conclusion of my historical research is that modern industrial growth did not change this basic fact as much as one might have expected. Of course, the growth rate following the Industrial Revolution rose, typically from zero to one to two percent, but at the same time, the rate of return to capital also rose so that the gap between the two did not really change. So, during the 20th century, you had a very unique combination of events. First, a very low rate of return due to the 1914 and 1945 war shocks, destruction of wealth, inflation, bankruptcy during the Great Depression, and all of this reduced the private rate of return to wealth to unusually low levels between 1914 and 1945. And then, in the postwar period, you had unusually high growth rate, partly due to the reconstruction. You know, in Germany, in France, in Japan, you had five percent growth rate between 1950 and 1980 largely due to reconstruction, and also due to very large demographic growth, the Baby Boom Cohort effect. Now, apparently that's not going to last for very long, or at least the population growth is supposed to decline in the future, and the best projections we have is that the long-run growth is going to be closer to one to two percent rather than four to five percent. So if you look at this, these are the best estimates we have of world GDP growth and rate of return on capital, average rates of return on capital, so you can see that during most of the history of mankind, the growth rate was very small, much lower than the rate of return, and then during the 20th century, it is really the population growth, very high in the postwar period, and the reconstruction process that brought growth to a smaller gap with the rate of return. Here I use the United Nations population projections, so of course they are uncertain. It could be that we all start having a lot of children in the future, and the growth rates are going to be higher, but from now on, these are the best projections we have, and this will make global growth decline and the gap between the rate of return go up.

Now, the other unusual event during the 20th century was, as I said, destruction, taxation of capital, so this is the pre-tax rate of return. This is the after-tax rate of return, and after destruction, and this is what brought the average rate of return after tax, after destruction, below the growth rate during a long time   period. But   without   the destruction, without the taxation, this would not have happened. So let me say that the balance between returns on capital and growth depends on many different factors that are very difficult to predict: technology and the development of capital-intensive techniques. So right now, the most capital-intensive sectors in the economy are the real estate sector, housing, the energy sector, but it could be in the future that we have a lot more robots in a number of sectors and that this would be a bigger share of the total capital stock that it is today. Well, we are very far from this, and from now, what's going on in the real estate sector, the energy sector, is much more important for the total capital stock and capital share.

The other important issue is that there are   scale   effects   in   portfolio management, together   with   financial complexity, financial deregulation, that make it easier to get higher rates of return for a large portfolio, and this seems to be particularly strong for billionaires, large capital endowments. Just to give you one example, this comes from the Forbes billionaire rankings over the 1987-2013 period, and you can see the very top wealth holders have been going up at six, seven percent per year in real terms above inflation, whereas average income in the world, average wealth in the world, have increased at only two percent per year. And you find the same for large university endowments — the bigger the initial endowments, the bigger the rate of return.

Now, what could be done? The first thing is that I think we need more financial transparency. We know too little about global wealth dynamics, so we need international transmission of bank information. We need a global registry of financial assets, more coordination on wealth taxation, and even wealth tax with a small tax rate will be a way to produce information so that then we can adapt our policies to whatever we observe. And to some extent, the fight against tax havens and automatic transmission of information is pushing us in this direction. Now, there are other ways to redistribute wealth, which it can be tempting to use. Inflation: it's much easier to print money than to write a tax code, so that's very tempting, but sometimes you don't know what you do with the money. This is a problem. Expropriation is very tempting. Just when you feel some people get too wealthy, you just expropriate them. But this is not a very efficient way to organize a regulation of wealth dynamics. So war is an even less efficient way, so I tend to prefer progressive taxation, but of course, history will invent its own best ways, and it will probably involve a combination of all of these.

Chapter 8
Bitcoin future of branded currency [8]

if I was to ask you what the connection between a bottle of Tide detergent and sweat was, you'd probably think that's the easiest question that you're going to be asked in Edinburgh all week. But if I was to say that they're both examples of alternative or new forms of currency in a hyperconnected, data-driven global economy, you'd probably think I was a little bit bonkers. But trust me, I work in advertising.

a more challenging question is one that I was asked, actually, by one of our writers a couple of weeks ago, and I didn't know the answer: What's the world's best performing currency? It's actually Bitcoin. Now, for those of you who may not be familiar, Bitcoin is a crypto-currency, a virtual currency, synthetic currency. It was founded in 2008 by this

---

[8] Paul Kemp Robertson: cofounder and editorial director of contagious communications.

anonymous programmer using a pseudonym Satoshi Nakamoto. No one knows who or what he is. He's almost liked the Banksy of the Internet.

And I'm probably not going to do it proper service here, but my interpretation of how it works is that Bitcoins are released through this process of mining. So, there's a network of computers that are challenged to solve a very complex mathematical problem and the person that manages to solve it first gets the Bitcoins. And the Bitcoins are released, they're put into a public ledger called the Blockchain, and then they float, so they become a currency, and completely decentralized, that's the sort of scary thing about this, which is why it's so popular. So, it's not run by the authorities or the state. It's actually managed by the network. And the reason that it's proved very successful is it's private, it's anonymous, it's fast, and it's cheap. And you do get to the point where there's some wild fluctuations with Bitcoin. So, in one level it went from something like 13 dollars to 266, literally in the space of four months, and then crashed and lost half of its value in six hours. And it's currently around that kind of 110-dollar mark in value.

But what it does show is that it's sort of gaining ground, it's gaining respectability. You get services, like Reddit and WordPress are actually accepting Bitcoin as a payment currency now. And that's showing you that people are actually placing trust in technology, and it's started to trump and disrupt and interrogate traditional institutions and how we think about currencies and money. And that's not surprising, if you think about the basket case that is the E.U. I think there was a Gallup survey out recently that said something like, in America, trust in banks is at an all-time low, it's something like 21 percent. And you can see here some photographs from London where

Barclays sponsored the city bike scheme, and some activists have done some nice piece of guerrilla marketing here and doctored the slogans. "Sub-prime pedaling." "Barclays takes you for a ride." These are the more polite ones I could share with you today. But you get the gist, so people have really started to sort of lose faith in institutions.

There's a P.R. company called Edelman, they do this very interesting survey every year precisely around trust and what people are thinking. And this is a global survey, so these numbers are global. And what's interesting is that you can see that hierarchy is having a bit of a wobble, and it's all about heterarchical now, so people trust people like themselves more than they trust corporations and governments. And if you look at these figures for the more developed markets like U.K., Germany, and so on, they're actually much lower. And I find that sort of scary. People are actually trusting businesspeople more than they're trusting governments and leaders.

So, what's starting to happen, if you think about money, if you sort of boil money down to an essence, it is literally just an expression of value, an agreed value. So, what's happening now, in the digital age, is that we can quantify value in lots of different ways and do it more easily, and sometimes the way that we quantify those values, it makes it much easier to create new forms and valid forms of currency. In that context, you can see that networks like Bitcoin suddenly start to make a bit more sense.

So, if you think we're starting to question and disrupt and interrogate what money means, what our relationship with it is, what defines money, then the ultimate extension of that is, is there a reason for the government to be in charge of money anymore? So obviously I'm looking at this through a marketing prism, so from a brand perspective, brands literally stand or fall on their reputations. And if you think about it, reputation has now become a currency. You know, reputations are built on trust, consistency, transparency. So if you've actually decided that you trust a brand, you want a relationship, you want to engage with the brand, you're already kind of participating in lots of new forms of currency.

So, you think about loyalty. Loyalty essentially is a micro-economy. You think about rewards schemes, air miles. The Economist said a few years ago that there are actually more unredeemed air miles in the world than there are dollar bills in circulation. You know, when you are standing in line in Starbucks, 30 percent of transactions in Starbucks on any one day are actually being made with Starbucks Star points. So that's a sort of Starbucks currency staying within its ecosystem.

And what I find interesting is that Amazon has recently launched Amazon coins. So admittedly it's a currency at the moment that's purely for the Kindle. So you can buy apps and make purchases within those apps, but you think about Amazon, you look at the trust barometer that I showed you where people are starting to trust businesses, especially businesses that they believe in and trust more than governments. So suddenly, you start thinking, well Amazon potentially could push this. It could become a natural extension, that as well as buying stuff -- take it out of the Kindle -- you could buy books, music, real-life products, appliances and goods and so on. And suddenly you're getting Amazon, as a brand, is going head to head with the Federal Reserve in terms of how you want to spend your money, what money is, what constitutes money.

And I'll get you back to Tide, the detergent now, as I promised. This is a fantastic article I came across in New York Magazine, where it was saying that drug users across America are actually purchasing drugs with bottles of Tide detergent. So, they're going into convenience stores, stealing Tide, and a $20 bottle of Tide is equal to 10 dollars of crack cocaine or weed. And what they're saying, so some criminologists have looked at this and they're saying, well, okay, Tide as a product sells at a premium. It's 50 percent above the category average. It's infused with a very complex cocktail of chemicals, so it smells very luxurious and very distinctive, and, being a Procter and Gamble brand, it's been supported by a lot of mass media advertising. So, what they're saying is that drug users are consumers too, so they have this in their neural pathways. When they spot Tide, there's a shortcut. They say, that is trust. I trust that. That's quality. So, it becomes this unit of currency, which the New York Magazine described as a very oddly loyal crime wave, brand-loyal crime wave, and criminals are actually calling Tide "liquid gold."

Now, what I thought was funny was the reaction from the P&G spokesperson. They said, obviously tried to dissociate themselves from drugs, but said, "It reminds me of one thing and that's the value of the brand has stayed consistent. Which backs up my point and shows he didn't even break a sweat when he said that.

So that brings me back to the connection with sweat. In Mexico, Nike has run a campaign recently called, literally, Bid Your Sweat. So, you think about, these Nike shoes have got sensors in them, or you're using a Nike FuelBand that basically tracks your movement, your energy, your calorie consumption. And what's happening here, this is where you've actually elected to join that Nike community. You've bought into it. They're not advertising loud messages at you, and that's where advertising has started to shift now is into things like services, tools and applications. So Nike is literally acting as a well-being partner, a health and fitness partner and service provider.

So, what happens with this is they're saying, "Right, you have a data dashboard. We know how far you've run, how far you've moved, what your calorie intake, all that sort of stuff. What you can do is, the more you run, the more points you get, and we have an auction where you can buy Nike stuff but only by proving that you've actually used the product to do stuff." And you can't come into this. This is purely for the community that are sweating using Nike products. You can't buy stuff with pesos. This is literally a closed environment, a closed auction space.

In Africa, you know, airtime has become literally a currency in its own right. People are used to, because mobile is king, they're very, very used to transferring money, making payments via mobile. And one of my favorite examples from a brand perspective going on is Vodafone, where, in

Egypt, lots of people make purchases in markets and very small independent stores. Loose change, small change is a real problem, and what tends to happen is you buy a bunch of stuff, you're due, say, 10 cents, 20 cents in change. The shopkeepers tend to give you things like an onion or an aspirin, or a piece of gum, because they don't have small change. So when Vodafone came in and saw this problem, this consumer pain point, they created some small change which they call Fakka, which literally sits and is given by the shopkeepers to people, and it's credit that goes straight onto their mobile phone. So, this currency becomes credit, which again, is really, really interesting.

And we did a survey that backs up the fact that, you know, 45 percent of people in this very crucial demographic in the U.S. were saying that they're comfortable using an independent or branded currency. So that's getting really interesting here, a really interesting dynamic going on. And you think, corporations should start taking their assets and thinking of them in a different way and trading them. And you think, is it much of a leap? It seems farfetched, but when you think about it, in America in 1860, there were 1,600 corporations issuing banknotes. There were 8,000 kinds of notes in America. And the only thing that stopped that, the government-controlled four percent of the supply, and the only thing that stopped it was the Civil War breaking out, and the government suddenly wanted to take control of the money. So, government, money, war, nothing changes there, then.

So, what I'm going to ask is, basically, is history repeating itself? Is technology making paper money feel outmoded? Are we decoupling money from the government? You know, you think about, brands are starting to fill the gaps. Corporations are filling gaps that governments can't afford to fill.

Chapter 9
The currency of the new economy
is trust [9]

if someone asked you for the three words that would sum up your reputation, what would you say? How would people describe your judgment, your knowledge, your behaviors, in different situations? Today I'd like to explore with you why the answer to this question will become profoundly important in an age where reputation will be your most valuable asset.

I'd like to start by introducing you to someone whose life has been changed by a marketplace fueled by reputation. Sebastian Sandys has been a bed and breakfast host on Airbnb since 2008. I caught up with him recently, where, over the course of several cups of tea, he told me how hosting guests from all over the world has enriched his life. More than

---

[9] Rachel Botsman: What's Mine Is Yours: The Rise of Collaborative Consumption, amazon 2010

50 people have come to stay in the 18th-century watchhouse he lives in with his cat, Squeak. Now, I mention Squeak because Sebastian's first guest happened to see a rather large mouse run across the kitchen, and she promised that she would refrain from leaving a bad review on one condition: he got a cat. And so Sebastian bought Squeak to protect his reputation.

Now, as many of you know, Airbnb is a peer-to-peer marketplace that matches people who have space to rent with people who are looking for a place to stay in over 192 countries. The places being rented out are things that you might expect, like spare rooms and holiday homes, but part of the magic is the unique places that you can now access: treehouses, teepees, airplane hangars, igloos. If you don't like the hotel, there's a castle down the road that you can rent for 5,000 dollars a night. It's a fantastic example of how technology is creating a market for things that never had a marketplace before.

Now let me show you these heat maps of Paris to see how insanely fast it's growing. This image here is from 2008. The pink dots represent host properties. Even four years ago, letting strangers stay in your home seemed like a crazy idea. Now the same view in 2010. And now, 2012. There is an Airbnb host on almost every main street in Paris. Now, what's happening here is people are realizing the power of technology to unlock the idling capacity and value of all kinds of assets, from skills to spaces to material possessions, in ways and on a scale never possible before. It's an economy and culture called collaborative consumption, and, through it, people like Sebastian are becoming micro-entrepreneurs. They're empowered to make money and save money from their existing assets.

But the real magic and the secret source behind collaborative consumption marketplaces like Airbnb isn't the inventory or the money. It's using the power of technology to build trust between strangers. This side of Airbnb really hit home to Sebastian last summer during the London riots. He woke up around 9, and he checked his email and he saw a bunch of messages all asking him if he was okay. Former guests from around the world had seen that the riots were happening just down the street, and wanted to check if he needed anything. Sebastian actually said to me, he said, "Thirteen former guests contacted me before my own mother rang.

Now, this little anecdote gets to the heart of why I'm really passionate about collaborative consumption, and why, after I finished my book, I decided I'm going to try and spread this into a global movement. Because at its core, it's about empowerment. It's about empowering people to make meaningful connections, connections that are enabling us to rediscover a humanness that we've lost somewhere along the way, by engaging in marketplaces like Airbnb, like Kickstarter, like Etsy, that are built on personal relationships versus empty transactions.

Now the irony is that these ideas are actually taking us back to old market principles and collaborative behaviors that are hard-wired in all of us. They're just being reinvented in ways that are relevant for the Facebook age. We're literally beginning to realize that we have wired our world to share, swap, rent, barter or trade just about anything. We're sharing our cars on WhipCar, our bikes on Spinlister, our offices on Loosecubes, our gardens on Landshare. We're lending and borrowing money from strangers on Zopa and Lending Club. We are trading lessons on everything from sushi-making to coding on Skillshare, and we're even sharing our pets on DogVacay. Now welcome to the wonderful world of collaborative consumption that's enabling us to match wants with haves in more democratic ways.

Now, collaborative consumption is creating the start of a transformation in the way we think about supply and demand, but it's also a part of a massive value shift underway, where instead of consuming to keep up with the Joneses, people are consuming to get to know the Joneses. But the key reason why it's taking off now so fast is because every new advancement of technology increases the efficiency and the social glue of trust to make sharing easier and easier.

Now, I've looked at thousands of these marketplaces, and trust and efficiency are always the critical ingredients. Let me give you an example. Meet 46-year-old Chris Mok, who has, I bet, the best job title here of SuperRabbit. Now, four years ago, Chris lost his job, unfortunately, as an art buyer at Macy's, and like so many people, he struggled to find a new one during the recession. And then he happened to stumble across a post about TaskRabbit.

Now, the story behind TaskRabbit starts like so many great stories with a very cute dog by the name of Kobe. Now what happened was, in February 2008, Leah and her husband were waiting for a cab to take them out for dinner, when Kobe came trotting up to them and he was salivating with saliva. They realized they'd run out of dog food. Kevin had to cancel the cab and trudge out in the snow. Now, later that evening, the two self-confessed tech geeks starting talking about how cool it would be if some kind of eBay for errands existed. Six months later, Leah quit her job, and TaskRabbit was born. At the time, she didn't realize that she was actually hitting on a bigger idea she later called service networking. It's essentially about how we use our online relationships to get things done in the real world.

Now the way TaskRabbit works is, people outsource the tasks that they want doing, name the price they're willing to pay, and then vetted Rabbits bid to run the errand. Yes, there's actually a four-stage, rigorous interview process that's designed to find the people that would make great personal assistants and weed out the dodgy Rabbits. Now, there's over 4,000 Rabbits across the United States and 5,000 more on the waiting list.

Now the tasks being posted are things that you might expect, like help with household chores or doing some supermarket runs. I actually learned the other day that 12 and a half thousand loads of laundry have been cleaned and folded through TaskRabbit. But I love that the number one task posted, over a hundred times a day, is something that many of us have felt the pain of doing: yes, assembling Ikea furniture. It's brilliant. Now, we may laugh, but Chris here is actually making up to 5,000 dollars a month running errands around his life. And 70 percent of this new labor force were previously unemployed or underemployed. I think TaskRabbit and other examples of collaborative consumption are like lemonade stands on steroids. They're just brilliant.

Now, when you think about it, it's amazing, right, that over the past 20 years, we've evolved from trusting people online to share information to trusting to handing over our credit card information, and now we're entering the third trust wave: connecting trustworthy strangers to create all kinds of people-powered marketplaces. I actually came across this fascinating study by the Pew Center this week that revealed that an active Facebook user is three times as likely as a non-Internet user to believe that most people are trustworthy. Virtual trust will transform the way we trust one another face to face.

Now, with all of my optimism, and I am an optimist, comes a healthy dose of caution, or rather, an urgent need to address some pressing, complex questions. How to ensure our digital identities reflect our real-world identities? Do we want them to be the same? How do we mimic the way trust is built face-to-face online? How do we stop people who've behaved badly in one community doing so under a different guise? In a similar way that companies often use some kind of credit rating to decide whether to give you a mobile plan, or the rate of a mortgage, marketplaces that depend on transactions between relative strangers need some kind of device to let you know that Sebastian and Chris are good eggs, and that device is reputation.

Reputation is the measurement of how much a community trusts you. Let's just take a look at Chris. You can see that over 200 people have given him an average rating over 4.99 out of 5. There are over 20 pages of reviews of his work describing him as super-friendly and fast, and he's reached level 25, the highest level, making him a SuperRabbit. Now — (Laughter) -- I love that word,

SuperRabbit. And interestingly, what Chris has noted is that as his reputation has gone up, so has his chances of winning a bid and how much he can charge. In other words, for SuperRabbits, reputation has a real-world value.

Now, I know what you might be thinking. Well, this isn't anything new. Just think of power sellers on eBay or star ratings on Amazon. The difference today is that, with every trade we make, comment we leave, person we flag, badge we earn, we leave a reputation trail of how well we can and can't be trusted. And it's not just the breadth but the volume of reputation data out there that is staggering. Just consider this: Five million nights have been booked on Airbnb in the past six months alone. 30 million rides have been shared on Carpooling.com. This year, two billion dollars' worth of loans will go through peer-to-peer lending platforms. This adds up to millions of pieces of reputation data on how well we behave or misbehave.

Now, capturing and correlating the trails of information that we leave in different places is a massive challenge, but one we're being asked to figure out. What the likes of Sebastian are starting to rightfully ask is, shouldn't they own their reputation data? Shouldn't the reputation that he's personally invested on building on Airbnb mean that it should travel with him from one community to another? What I mean by this is, say he started selling second-hand books on Amazon. Why should he have to start from scratch? It's a bit like when I moved from New York to Sydney. It was ridiculous. I couldn't get a mobile phone plan because my credit history didn't travel with me. I was essentially a ghost in the system.

Now I'm not suggesting that the next stage of the reputation economy is about adding up multiple ratings into some kind of empty score. People's lives are too complex, and who wants to do that? I also want to be clear that this isn't about adding up tweets and likes and friends in a Klout-like fashion. Those guys are measuring influence, not behaviors that indicate our trustworthiness.

But the most important thing that we have to keep in mind is that reputation is largely contextual. Just because Sebastian is a wonderful host does not mean that he can assemble Ikea furniture. The big challenge is figuring out what data makes sense to pull, because the future's going to be driven by a smart aggregation of reputation, not a single algorithm. It's only a matter of time before we'll be able to perform a Facebook- or Google-like search and see a complete picture of someone's behaviors in different contexts over time.

I envision a real-time stream of who has trusted you, when, where and why, your reliability on TaskRabbit, your cleanliness as a guest on Airbnb, the knowledge that you display on Quora or Tripovo, they'll all live together in one place, and this will live in some kind of reputation dashboard that will paint a picture of your reputation capital.

Now this is a concept that I'm currently researching and writing my next book on, and currently define as the worth of your reputation, your intentions, capabilities and values across communities and marketplaces.

This isn't some far-off frontier. There is actually a wave of startups like Connect.Me and Legit and TrustCloud that are figuring out how you can aggregate, monitor and use your online reputation.

Now, I realize that this concept may sound a little Big Brother to some of you, and yes, there are some enormous transparency and privacy issues to solve, but ultimately, if we can collect our personal reputation, we can actually control it more, and extract the immense value that will flow from it.

Also, more so than our credit history, we can actually shape our reputation. Just think of Sebastian and how he bought the cat to influence his.

Now privacy issues aside, the other really interesting issue I'm looking at is how do we empower digital ghosts, people [who] for whatever reason, are not active online, but are some of the most trustworthy people in the world? How do we take their contributions to their jobs, their communities and their families, and convert that value into reputation capital?

Ultimately, when we get it right, reputation capital could create a massive positive disruption in who has power, trust and influence.

A three-digit score, your traditional credit history, that only 30 percent of us actually know what it is, will no longer be the determining factor in how much things cost, what we can access, and, in many instances, limit what we can do in the world. Indeed, reputation is a currency that I believe will become more powerful than our credit history in the 21st century. Reputation will be the currency that says that you can trust me.

Now the interesting thing is, reputation is the socioeconomic lubricant that makes collaborative consumption work and scale, but the sources it will be generated from, and its applications, are far bigger than this space alone.

Let me give you one example from the world of recruiting, where reputation data will make the résumé seem like an archaic relic of the past.

Four years ago, tech bloggers and entrepreneurs Joel Spolsky and Jeff Atwood, decided to start something called Stack Overflow. Now, Stack Overflow is basically a platform where experienced programmers can ask other good programmers highly detailed technical questions on things like tiny pixels and chrome extensions.

This site receives five and a half thousand questions a day, and 80 percent of these receive accurate answers. Now users earn reputation in a whole range of ways, but it's basically by convincing their peers they know what they're talking about.

a few months after this site launched, the founders heard about something interesting, and it actually didn't surprise them. What they heard was that users were putting their reputation scores on the top of their résumés, and that recruiters were searching the platform to find people with unique talents.

Now thousands of programmers today are finding better jobs this way, because Stack Overflow and the reputation dashboards provide a priceless window into how someone really behaves, and what their peers think of them.

But the bigger principle of what's happening behind Stack Overflow, I think, is incredibly exciting. People are starting to realize that the reputation they generate in one place has value beyond the environments from which it was built. You know, it's very interesting.

When you talk to super-users, whether that's SuperRabbits or super-people on Stack Overflow, or Uberhosts, they all talk about how having a high reputation unlocks a sense of their own power. On Stack Overflow, it creates a level playing field, enabling the people with the real talent to rise to the top. On Airbnb, the people often become more important than the spaces. On TaskRabbit, it gives people control of their economic activity.

Now at the end of my tea with Sebastian, he told me how, on a bad, rainy day, when he hasn't had a customer in his bookstore, he thinks of all the people around the world who've said something wonderful about him, and what that says about him as a person.

He's turning 50 this year, and he's convinced that the rich tapestry of reputation he's built on Airbnb will lead him to doing something interesting with the rest of his life.

You know, there are only a few windows in history where the opportunity exists to reinvent part of how our socioeconomic system works.

We're living through one of those moments. I believe that we are at the start of a collaborative revolution that will be as significant as the Industrial Revolution. In the 20th century, the invention of traditional credit transformed our consumer system, and in many ways controlled who had access to what. In the 21st century, new trust networks, and the reputation capital they generate, will reinvent the way we think about wealth, markets, power and personal identity, in ways we can't yet even imagine. Thank you very much.

References

1. Chrystia Freeland: plutocracy chronicle.

2. Suhas Ketkar, Dilip Ratha: Innovative Financing for Development, amazon, 2008.

3. Didier Sornette: risk economist

4. Mariana Mazzucato: The Value of Everything: Making and Taking in the Global Economy 2nd Edition, penguin, 2019.

5. Thomas Piketty: Capital in the Twenty First Century, amazon, 2014

6. Adam Davidson: co-host and co-creator of planet money.

7. Paul Kemp Robertson: cofounder and editorial director of contagious communications

8. Rachel Botsman: What's Mine Is Yours: The Rise of Collaborative Consumption, amazon 2010

9. kate raworth: renegade economist.

www.ingramcontent.com/pod-product-compliance
Lightning Source LLC
Chambersburg PA
CBHW030651220526
45463CB00005B/1732